PIZZA
AND
ANTIPASTI

BRIMAR

Editor Angela Rahaniotis
Graphic Design Zapp
Photography Marc Bruneau
Food Preparation / Stylist Josée Robitaille
Assistant Stylist Marc Maula

©1994 Brimar Publishing Inc.
338 Saint Antoine St. East
Montreal, Canada H2Y 1A3
Tel. (514) 954-1441
Fax (514) 954-5086

ISBN 2-89433-121-5
Printed in Canada

PIZZA
AND
ANTIPASTI

Everybody loves pizza! But many home cooks think pizza is too complicated to make from scratch.

This cookbook will show you otherwise, with easy, step-by-step recipes for pizza dough and an exciting variety of sauces and toppings that will turn you into an expert in no time at all.

In addition, this book contains a wonderful selection of delicious antipasti – the Italian approach to starters and snacks. Your family and friends will rave over these flavor-packed and healthy salads, dips, marinated vegetables, and hors d'oeuvres.

And with the full-color photographs accompanying each recipe, you will be able to turn out antipasti and pizzas that will tantalize the eye as well as the tastebuds.

Bruschetta
(6 to 10 servings)

¼ cup	extra virgin olive oil	50 mL
2	large tomatoes, peeled, seeded and chopped	2
2 tbsp	chopped fresh basil	30 mL
3	garlic cloves, peeled, crushed and sliced	3
8	anchovy fillets, drained	8
10	slices toasted French baguette	10
	salt and pepper	

1 Heat half of olive oil in frying pan over high heat. Add tomatoes and basil; season and cook 4 minutes. Remove pan from heat.

2 Heat remaining oil in small saucepan. Add garlic and anchovy fillets; cook 2 minutes.

3 Place about 1 tbsp (15 mL) of tomato mixture on each slice of bread. Top with garlic and anchovy fillets. Season well with pepper and serve.

Hot Chicken Croquettes
(4 to 6 servings)

2 cups	cooked chicken, diced small	500 mL
1 ½ cups	White Sauce, heated (see p. 38)	375 mL
2	slices cooked ham, minced	2
4 tbsp	grated Parmesan cheese	60 mL
3	eggs	3
1 tsp	extra virgin olive oil	5 mL
1 ½ cups	white breadcrumbs	375 mL
	salt and freshly ground pepper	
	few drops of hot pepper sauce	
	pinch of nutmeg	
	oil for deep frying	

1 Place chicken, white sauce, ham, cheese and 1 egg in bowl. Mix together and season well. Add hot pepper sauce and pinch of nutmeg. If preferred, mixture can be prepared in food processor.

2 Refrigerate mixture 15 minutes.

3 Shape chilled mixture into small croquettes. Beat remaining eggs with extra virgin olive oil. Dip croquettes in beaten eggs, then roll in breadcrumbs.

4 Deep fry in hot oil until nicely browned. Serve with spicy sauce.

Broccoli and Cauliflower Insalata
(6 servings)

1	head broccoli, in small florets	1
1	small head cauliflower, in florets	1
1	small zucchini, sliced	1
1	red bell pepper, chopped	1
6	artichoke hearts, marinated in oil	6
½ cup	pitted Kalamata olives	125 mL
6	anchovy fillets, drained and chopped	6
6	garlic cloves, blanched, peeled and puréed	6
1 tbsp	chopped fresh parsley	15 mL
1 tbsp	chopped fresh basil	15 mL
⅓ cup	olive oil	75 mL
2 oz	Gorgonzola cheese, crumbled	60 g
	juice of 1½ lemons	
	salt and pepper	

1 Blanch broccoli in boiling salted water for 2 minutes. Remove from pan and place immediately under cold, running water. Drain and set aside.

2 Add cauliflower and zucchini to boiling water. Blanch 3 minutes. Place vegetables under cold, running water. Drain and set aside.

3 Place broccoli, cauliflower, zucchini and chopped bell pepper in large bowl. Slice artichoke hearts in half and add to bowl. Toss in olives and mix well.

4 Place anchovies in small bowl. Add garlic, herbs and lemon juice; whisk together. Pour in oil and whisk until incorporated. Season dressing with pepper and pour over salad ingredients.

5 Toss salad, correct seasoning and marinate 20 minutes at room temperature. Sprinkle with cheese before serving.

Blanch broccoli in boiling salted water for 2 minutes. Remove from pan and place immediately under cold, running water. Drain and set aside.

Add cauliflower and zucchini to boiling water. Blanch 3 minutes. Place vegetables under cold, running water. Drain and set aside.

Slice artichoke hearts in half and add to bowl. Toss in olives and mix well.

Place anchovies in small bowl. Add garlic, herbs and lemon juice; whisk together. Pour in oil and whisk until incorporated. Season dressing with pepper and pour over salad ingredients.

Eggs à la Grecque
(4 servings)

3	leeks, white part only	3
24	white pearl onions, peeled	24
1 lb	fresh mushroom caps, cleaned	450 g
4	garlic cloves, peeled	4
1 1/2 cups	dry white wine	375 mL
1/2 cup	water	125 mL
2 tbsp	tomato paste	30 mL
2	bay leaves	2
4	fresh basil leaves	4
12	black peppercorns	12
1/4 tsp	thyme	1 mL
4	cold poached eggs	4
	juice of 1/2 lemon	
	salt and pepper	

1 Slit leeks from top to bottom twice, leaving 1 in (2.5 cm) intact at base. Wash leeks under cold, running water to remove grit and sand. Slice thinly.

2 Place leeks in boiling salted water. Add a few drops of lemon juice and cook 6 minutes over medium heat. Remove leeks and drain well.

3 Transfer leeks to saucepan and add remaining ingredients, except eggs. Cook 15 minutes over low heat.

4 Serve leek mixture over cold poached eggs.

Cauliflower and Hard-Boiled Eggs
(4 to 6 servings)

1	large cauliflower, in florets and blanched	1
8	anchovy fillets, drained and chopped	8
¾ cup	pitted black olives, sliced	175 mL
3 tbsp	capers	45 mL
2 tbsp	chopped fresh basil	30 mL
4 tbsp	balsamic vinegar	60 mL
½ cup	extra virgin olive oil	125 mL
2	hard-boiled eggs, quartered	2
	salt and pepper	

1 Place blanched cauliflower in bowl. Add anchovies, olives and capers. Season well and add basil; mix carefully.

2 Place vinegar, salt and pepper in separate bowl. Add olive oil and whisk together.

3 Pour vinaigrette over salad and toss lightly. Marinate 15 minutes. Serve garnished with hard-boiled eggs.

Mozzarella au Gratin
(6 to 8 servings)

6	slices Italian bread, 1/3 in (8 mm) thick	6
1 1/2 cups	milk	375 mL
1 1/2 cups	grated mozzarella cheese	375 mL
2 tbsp	flour	30 mL
2	large eggs, beaten	2
3 tbsp	olive oil	45 mL
3 tbsp	butter	45 mL
	salt and pepper	

1 Remove crusts from bread. Dip slices of bread in milk.

2 Divide cheese among 3 slices of bread. Season well and cover with remaining bread to make sandwiches. Cut sandwiches in half.

3 Sprinkle flour over sandwiches, then dip each in beaten eggs.

4 Heat oil and butter in large frying pan over medium heat. Fry sandwiches 2 to 3 minutes on each side or until cheese is melted and sandwiches are nicely browned.

5 Blot sandwiches on paper towel, then cut into small squares. Serve hot.

Stuffed Zucchini
(4 to 6 servings)

3	**zucchini**	3
3	**large yellow bell peppers**	3
¼ cup	**olive oil**	50 mL
4	**large tomatoes, peeled, seeded and chopped**	4
2	**garlic cloves, peeled, crushed and chopped**	2
3 tbsp	**chopped fresh basil**	45 mL
12	**slices Caciocavallo cheese**	12
	salt and pepper	
	few drops of extra virgin olive oil	

Preheat oven to 400°F (200°C).

1 Slice zucchini in half lengthwise. Using melon baller, scoop out most of zucchini flesh, leaving shell intact. Place zucchini shells in boiling water for 1 minute. Remove and set aside to drain.

2 Cut bell peppers in half and remove seeds. Oil skin and place cut-side-down on cookie sheet; broil 6 to 8 minutes in oven. Remove from oven and place in large bowl. Cover bowl with plastic wrap. Let peppers steam 3 minutes. Peel and discard skins. Slice peppers thinly.

3 Heat oil in sauté pan over medium heat. Add tomatoes, garlic and basil; season well. Cook 10 minutes.

4 Arrange zucchini shells in baking dish. Fill with tomato mixture and cover with slices of cheese. Drizzle few drops of extra virgin olive oil over cheese.

5 Broil 2 minutes in oven, or until cheese melts.

Shrimp Cheese Spread
(6 to 10 servings)

3 tbsp	olive oil	45 mL
1 lb	fresh shrimp, peeled, deveined and quartered	450 g
3	shallots, peeled and chopped	3
2	garlic cloves, peeled, crushed and chopped	2
1	small chili pepper, seeded and chopped	1
½ lb	cream cheese	225 g
2 oz	pimiento pepper, chopped	60 g
	salt and pepper	
	few drops of lime juice	

1 Heat oil in frying pan over medium heat. Add shrimp, shallots, garlic and chili pepper; season well. Cook 4 minutes, stirring once.

2 Cool, then transfer mixture to food processor. Blend several seconds and add remaining ingredients. Blend until combined. Correct seasoning.

3 Serve on toasted bread or crackers or as a stuffing for celery stalks.

Anchovy and Garlic Dip
(6 to 10 servings)

4 cups	heavy cream	1 L
12	anchovy fillets, drained and finely chopped	12
4	garlic cloves, peeled, crushed and finely chopped	4
	salt and freshly ground pepper	
	cayenne pepper to taste	

1 Pour cream into saucepan, season and bring to boil. Cook over low heat until reduced by half.

2 Add anchovies and garlic. Simmer 6 minutes.

3 Pour into fondue dish and keep warm while serving.

Use this dip for fresh vegetables and toasted bread sticks.

Sicilian Ratatouille
(6 to 8 servings)

2	large eggplants, cubed	2
½ cup	olive oil	125 mL
3	onions, peeled and sliced	3
3	garlic cloves, peeled, crushed and chopped	3
4	large tomatoes, peeled, seeded and chopped	4
3 tbsp	capers	45 mL
½ cup	pitted olives	125 mL
3 tbsp	white wine vinegar	45 mL
1 tbsp	honey	15 mL
	salt and pepper	

1 Spread cubes of eggplant in one layer in large container. Sprinkle with salt and let stand 40 minutes at room temperature. Drain well and set eggplant aside.

2 Heat ¼ cup (50 mL) oil in large frying pan over medium heat. Add onions and cook 18 minutes over low heat. Do not let burn.

3 Add garlic, tomatoes, capers and season well. Continue cooking 10 minutes. Stir in olives.

4 Heat remaining oil in separate large frying pan over medium heat. Add eggplant, season and cook 15 minutes.

5 Incorporate tomato mixture to eggplant. Add vinegar and honey. Mix well and correct seasoning. Continue cooking 16 minutes to evaporate all liquid.

6 Serve cold on small rounds of toasted bread.

Toasted Italian Bread with Marinated Tomatoes
(6 servings)

3	garlic cloves, blanched, peeled and puréed	3
3 tbsp	extra virgin olive oil	45 mL
2	large tomatoes, peeled, seeded and coarsely chopped	2
2 tbsp	chopped fresh basil	30 mL
6	thick slices Italian bread	6
6	slices Fontina cheese	6
8	anchovy fillets, drained and chopped	8
	salt and freshly ground pepper	

Preheat oven to 350°F (180°C).

1 Place garlic in mixing bowl. Add olive oil and whisk together to incorporate. Add tomatoes and basil; mix well. Season and marinate 30 minutes at room temperature.

2 Arrange slices of Italian bread on cookie sheet. Divide cheese among slices and top with chopped anchovies. Season with pepper.

3 Cook 6 minutes in oven or until cheese melts.

4 Using slotted spoon, top each portion with marinated tomato mixture. Season with freshly ground pepper and serve.

Celeriac Remoulade
(4 to 6 servings)

1	large celeriac, peeled and shredded	1
1	large egg yolk	1
1 tbsp	Dijon mustard	15 mL
3	garlic cloves, blanched, peeled and puréed	3
1 tbsp	lemon juice	15 mL
½ cup	olive oil	125 mL
1 tbsp	chopped fresh parsley	15 mL
	juice of 1 lemon	
	salt and pepper	
	lettuce leaves	

1 Cook shredded celeriac in salted, lemony boiling water for 5 minutes. Place under cold, running water to stop cooking process. Drain and squeeze out excess liquid.

2 Place celeriac in large bowl with juice of 1 lemon. Mix, cover bowl and set aside.

3 Place egg yolk, mustard, garlic and 1 tbsp (15 mL) lemon juice in small bowl. Season with salt and pepper. Whisk ingredients together.

4 Add oil in thin stream while whisking constantly. If mixture becomes too thick, add more lemon juice. Pour over celeriac; mix well. Add parsley, season and serve on lettuce leaves.

Pesto on Baguette
(6 to 8 servings)

1 cup	fresh basil, washed and dried	250 mL
1 cup	fresh curly parsley, washed and dried	250 mL
1 cup	fresh Italian parsley, washed and dried	250 mL
5	garlic cloves, peeled	5
¾ cup	grated Parmesan cheese	175 mL
¼ cup	pine nuts	50 mL
½ cup	olive oil	125 mL
⅓ cup	mayonnaise	75 mL
2	French baguettes	2
	few drops of lime juice	
	salt and freshly ground pepper	
	cayenne pepper to taste	
	grated mozzarella cheese (optional)	

1 Place basil, all parsley and garlic in food processor. Blend several seconds. Add Parmesan cheese and pine nuts; blend again to incorporate.

2 Add oil through hole in top while blending. Mixture should be fully incorporated. Transfer to bowl and stir in mayonnaise and lime juice. Season well with salt, pepper and cayenne pepper.

3 Cut baguettes in half lengthwise and broil in oven until lightly toasted. Remove and let cool.

4 Spread pesto over baguettes and broil 1 minute in oven. If desired, top bread with grated mozzarella cheese and broil 1 more minute. Slice and serve warm.

Braised Whole Leeks
(serves 4 to 6)

2 lb	leeks, white part only	900 g
1 cup	dry white wine	250 mL
1 cup	water	250 mL
½ cup	olive oil	125 mL
3	garlic cloves, peeled	3
12	peppercorns	12
1	bay leaf	1
1	sprig fresh thyme	1
6	fresh basil leaves	6
	juice of 2 lemons	
	salt and pepper	

1 Slit leeks from top to bottom twice, leaving 1 in (2.5 cm) intact at base. Wash leeks under cold, running water to remove grit and sand.

2 Place leeks and all ingredients in sauté pan over medium heat. Bring to boil.

3 Cook 35 minutes over low heat. When cooked, remove from heat and let leeks cool in marinade.

4 Serve leeks with some of the marinade.

Spicy Scallops
(4 servings)

2 tbsp	olive oil	30 mL
¾ lb	fresh scallops, cleaned and sliced	350 g
2 tbsp	chopped fresh basil	30 mL
2	garlic cloves, peeled, crushed and chopped	2
1	jalapeño pepper, seeded and chopped	1
½ lb	fresh mushrooms, cleaned and halved	225 g
24	seedless cucumber balls	24
3 tbsp	balsamic vinegar	45 mL
9 tbsp	extra virgin olive oil	135 mL
	salt and pepper	
	lettuce leaves	

1 Heat oil in frying pan over medium heat. Add scallops and increase heat to high. Cook 1 minute on each side. Add basil, garlic, jalapeño pepper and season well. Cook 1 more minute.

2 Remove scallops from pan and set aside in bowl. Add mushrooms to hot pan and cook 3 minutes over high heat. Add more oil if needed.

3 Add mushrooms to scallops in bowl. Mix in cucumber.

4 Mix vinegar with extra virgin olive oil; season well. Pour over salad, toss to incorporate and serve on lettuce leaves.

Braised Fennel in Olive Oil
(4 to 6 servings)

3	large fennel bulbs	3
½ cup	olive oil	125 mL
3	garlic cloves, peeled	3
1	sprig fresh thyme	1
12	fresh basil leaves	12
12	peppercorns	12
2	bay leaves	2
1	chili pepper, seeded and sliced	1
	juice of 1 lemon	
	salt and pepper	
	water	
	lemon wedges	
	chopped fresh basil	
	lettuce leaves	

1 Remove stems and green leaves from fennel bulbs. Peel bulbs and cut in half lengthwise. Slice into strips.

2 Place fennel in sauté pan. Add all ingredients, except lemon, chopped basil and lettuce leaves, with just enough water to cover. Season and bring to boil.

3 Cook 30 minutes over low heat or until tender. Do not cover. If liquid evaporates too quickly, replenish as needed.

4 Let cool in marinade. Serve on lettuce leaves with some of the marinade. Garnish with fresh lemon wedges and chopped basil, if desired.

Prosciutto with Stuffed Figs

(4 servings)

8	fresh figs, cut in half	8
1 tbsp	candied mixed fruit	15 mL
1 tbsp	honey	15 mL
1/3 cup	chopped mixed nuts	75 mL
1/2-3/4 lb	prosciutto	225-350 g
	lemon slices	

1 Scoop out 1 tsp (5 mL) of flesh from each fig half. Place flesh in bowl and add candied fruit and honey; mix well. Add mixed nuts and mix again. Stuff figs.

2 Arrange slices of prosciutto decoratively on serving platter. Position stuffed figs and garnish with lemon slices.

Tuna and White Beans
(4 to 6 servings)

2	19 oz (540 mL) cans, white beans, drained	2
¼ cup	olive oil	50 mL
1 tbsp	lemon juice	15 mL
3	green onions, chopped	3
2	garlic cloves, peeled, crushed and chopped	2
2 tbsp	chopped fresh Italian parsley	30 mL
1 tbsp	chopped fresh basil	15 mL
6.5 oz	can tuna, packed in oil, well drained	184 g
	salt and pepper	
	lettuce leaves	

1 Place beans in mixing bowl.

2 Pour oil into small bowl and add lemon juice; season well. Add green onions and garlic. Mix well. Add parsley and basil; mix again.

3 Pour vinaigrette over beans and mix well. Flake tuna and add to bowl. Mix, correct seasoning and serve salad on lettuce leaves.

Cooked Marinated Mushroom Caps
(4 to 6 servings)

¼ cup	dry white wine	50 mL
½ cup	olive oil	125 mL
2 tbsp	water	30 mL
2	bay leaves	2
4	garlic cloves	4
12	peppercorns	12
6	fresh basil leaves	6
1	sprig fresh thyme	1
1 lb	small fresh mushroom caps, cleaned	450 g
	juice of 1 lemon	
	salt and freshly ground pepper	
	cayenne pepper to taste	

1 Place all ingredients, except mushrooms, in saucepan. Bring to boil and cook 10 minutes over medium heat.

2 Add mushrooms to saucepan, season and mix. Cook 6 to 8 minutes over low heat.

3 Let mushrooms cool in marinade. Serve.

Salad of Mussels and Artichoke Hearts
(4 servings)

3 lb	fresh mussels, cleaned and bearded	1.4 kg
1/2 cup	dry white wine	125 mL
1	shallot, peeled and chopped	1
1 tbsp	chopped fresh parsley	15 mL
15	artichoke hearts, marinated in oil	15
4	fresh basil leaves	4
1/2 cup	pitted black olives	125 mL
3 oz	feta cheese, diced	90 g
3 tbsp	wine vinegar	45 mL
1/2 cup	olive oil	125 mL
1/4 tsp	oregano	1 mL
	salt and pepper	
	lettuce leaves	

1 Place mussels in saucepan with wine, shallot and parsley. Cover and cook 4 minutes over medium heat or until shells open. Discard any unopened shells.

2 Remove mussels from shells and place in mixing bowl. Drain artichokes and cut in quarters; add to bowl. Mix in basil leaves, olives and feta cheese. Season well.

3 Place vinegar, salt, pepper and oregano in separate bowl. Add oil and whisk together to incorporate. Pour over mussels and mix well. Correct seasoning and serve on lettuce leaves.

Artichokes, Italian Style
(4 to 6 servings)

12	very small fresh artichokes	12
I cup	dry white wine	250 mL
½ cup	olive oil	125 mL
½ cup	water	125 mL
12	peppercorns	12
12	small shallots, peeled	12
I	bay leaf	I
2	garlic cloves, peeled	2
	juice of 1 ½ lemons	
	salt and pepper	

1 Place all ingredients in saucepan. Bring to boil.

2 Cook artichokes 45 minutes over low heat. If liquid evaporates too quickly, replenish with combination of wine and water.

3 When artichokes are cooked, remove from heat and let cool in marinade.

4 Serve artichokes with some of marinade. Do not strain.

5 Accompany with fresh tomato sauce, if desired.

Eggplant Croustade
(6 to 8 servings)

¼ cup	olive oil	50 mL
1	onion, peeled and chopped	1
3	garlic cloves, peeled, crushed and chopped	3
1	small eggplant, diced	1
3	tomatoes, peeled, seeded and chopped	3
¼ tsp	crushed chilies	1 mL
2 tbsp	chopped fresh basil	30 mL
12	slices Italian bread, toasted	12
12	anchovy fillets, drained	12
12	slices Scamorze cheese	12
	freshly ground pepper	
	few drops of extra virgin olive oil	

1 Heat oil in sauté pan over medium heat. Add onion and garlic; cook 4 minutes over low heat.

2 Add eggplant, tomatoes and seasonings. Cook 20 minutes over medium heat.

3 Let mixture cool to room temperature, then spread over toasted bread. Top with anchovy fillets and cheese. Drizzle a few drops of extra virgin olive oil over cheese. Season generously with pepper. Broil 3 minutes and serve.

Tomatoes with Bocconcini
(4 servings)

2	bunches fresh basil	2
4	medium tomatoes	4
24	large cubes of Bocconcini cheese	24
¹⁄₄ cup	balsamic vinegar	50 mL
¹⁄₂ cup	olive oil	125 mL
	salt and freshly ground pepper	

1 Remove stems from fresh basil. Wash leaves and dry well.

2 Core tomatoes and cut in wedges. Place in mixing bowl with cheese and remaining ingredients, including fresh basil. Mix and marinate 30 minutes at room temperature.

3 Spoon tomatoes, cheese and basil on serving platter. Pour juices from bowl over ingredients. Serve.

White Bean and Shrimp Mélange
(4 to 6 servings)

3 tbsp	olive oil	45 mL
1	red onion, peeled and sliced in rings	1
½	celery stalk, sliced	½
2	garlic cloves, peeled and minced	2
1 lb	fresh shrimp, peeled and deveined	450 g
¼ tsp	crushed chilies	1 mL
2 oz	pimiento pepper, chopped	60 g
1 ¼ cups	cooked white beans	375 mL
3 tbsp	lemon juice	45 mL
6 tbsp	extra virgin olive oil	90 mL
2 tbsp	chopped fresh basil	30 mL
	salt and pepper	

1 Heat 3 tbsp (45 mL) olive oil in frying pan over medium heat. Add onion, celery and garlic; season well. Cook 6 minutes over low heat.

2 Add shrimp and crushed chilies. Increase heat to high and cook 3 to 4 minutes, stirring occasionally.

3 Transfer mixture to bowl. Add pimiento and white beans; season well. Mix in lemon juice and extra virgin olive oil. Add basil, mix and marinate 15 minutes at room temperature.

Balsamic Marinated Mushrooms
(4 to 6 servings)

1 lb	fresh mushrooms, cleaned and thinly sliced	450 g
3	green onions, chopped	3
3 tbsp	balsamic vinegar	45 mL
½ cup	olive oil	125 mL
1 tbsp	chopped fresh basil	15 mL
	juice of 2 lemons	
	salt and pepper	

1 Place mushrooms in mixing bowl. Add lemon juice, mixing to moisten all mushrooms. Add green onions.

2 Mix vinegar, oil, salt and pepper together in small bowl. Pour over mushrooms and mix well. Add basil and mix again.

3 Cover and marinate 1 hour in refrigerator. Serve mushrooms with some of the marinade.

Salad of Potatoes, Beans and Seafood
(4 to 6 servings)

3	potatoes, boiled unpeeled	3
¼ lb	cooked white beans	125 g
½ cup	sliced pitted black olives	125 mL
6 tbsp	extra virgin olive oil	90 mL
2	garlic cloves, peeled, crushed and chopped	2
2 tsp	chopped fresh parsley	10 mL
2 tsp	chopped fresh basil	10 mL
3	anchovy fillets, drained and chopped	3
2 tbsp	capers	30 mL
½ lb	fresh shrimp, cooked, shelled and deveined	225 g
3 oz	cooked crabmeat	90 g
	juice of 1 or 2 lemons	
	salt and pepper	
	cayenne pepper to taste	

1 Peel potatoes and cut in half. Place in bowl with beans and olives. Set aside.

2 Heat olive oil in frying pan over medium heat. Add garlic, parsley, basil and anchovies. Cook 1 minute. Add capers and lemon juice to taste; season well. Cook 30 seconds.

3 Stir and pour hot mixture over salad ingredients. Mix well and correct seasoning. Add cayenne pepper to taste.

4 Add shrimp and crabmeat. Mix and marinate 30 minutes at room temperature before serving.

Grilled Bell Peppers and Tomatoes
(4 to 6 servings)

6	bell peppers	6
¼ cup	extra virgin olive oil	50 mL
4	tomatoes, cored and sliced	4
2	garlic cloves, peeled and thinly sliced	2
8	anchovy fillets, drained and chopped	8
8	fresh basil leaves	8
	salt and pepper	

1 Cut bell peppers in half and remove seeds. Oil skin and place cut-side-down on cookie sheet; broil 10 minutes in oven. Remove from oven and let cool. Peel and discard skins. Slice peppers thinly.

2 Arrange sliced grilled peppers on serving platter; drizzle with some of the olive oil. Cover with sliced tomatoes.

3 Add garlic and anchovy fillets; season well. Drizzle with remaining oil and top with basil leaves. Marinate 18 minutes at room temperature before serving.

Fresh Mussels with Dolcelatte Cheese
(4 to 6 servings)

2 lb	fresh mussels, scrubbed and bearded	900 g
¼ cup	dry white wine	50 mL
2 cups	cooked white beans	500 mL
2	shallots, peeled and chopped	2
2	garlic cloves, peeled, crushed and chopped	2
2 tbsp	chopped fresh basil	30 mL
1 tbsp	capers	15 mL
1 tbsp	Italian mustard	15 mL
¼ cup	extra virgin olive oil	50 mL
3 oz	Dolcelatte cheese, crumbled	90 g
	salt and freshly ground pepper	
	lemon juice	

1 Place mussels in saucepan with wine. Cover and cook 5 to 6 minutes over medium heat, or until shells open.

2 Discard any unopened shells. Remove mussels from shells and transfer to bowl. Add white beans, shallots, garlic, basil and capers; season well.

3 Mix mustard, olive oil and lemon juice to taste together in separate bowl. Pour mixture over mussels and mix well.

4 Add cheese, mix and let marinate 15 minutes before serving.

Grilled Yellow Pepper Antipasto
(4 to 6 servings)

6	yellow bell peppers	6
3 oz	Fontina cheese, cut in julienne	90 g
½ cup	pitted green olives	125 mL
¼ cup	extra virgin olive oil	50 mL
1 tbsp	Dijon mustard	15 mL
2 tbsp	heavy cream	30 mL
	salt and freshly ground pepper	
	lettuce leaves	

1 Cut bell peppers in half and remove seeds. Oil skin and place cut-side-down on cookie sheet; broil 6 to 8 minutes in oven. Remove from oven and place in large bowl. Cover bowl with plastic wrap. Let peppers steam 3 minutes. Peel and discard skins. Slice peppers thinly.

2 Place bell peppers in bowl with all remaining ingredients. Mix well and correct seasoning.

3 Marinate 30 minutes at room temperature. Serve on lettuce leaves.

How to Peel and Seed Fresh Tomatoes

1 Core fresh tomatoes.

2 Place briefly in pot with boiling water, just long enough to loosen skins.

3 Remove tomatoes from pot and set aside to cool slightly. When cool enough to handle, peel off skins.

4 Slice tomatoes in half, horizontally. Grasp tomato half in hand, with cut side facing down. Squeeze out seeds into bowl.

5 Chop or dice tomatoes.

Basic Fresh Tomato Sauce

5	tomatoes, cored	5
2 tbsp	olive oil	30 mL
1	onion, peeled and chopped	1
3	garlic cloves, peeled, crushed and chopped	3
1 cup	dry white wine	250 mL
3 tbsp	chopped fresh basil	45 mL
1	small chili pepper, seeded and chopped	1
	salt and pepper	

1 Plunge tomatoes in saucepan with boiling water. Remove tomatoes after 1 minute. When cool enough to handle, remove skins. Cut tomatoes in half, horizontally and squeeze out seeds. Chop pulp and set aside.

2 Heat oil in sauté pan over medium heat. Add onion and garlic; cook 4 minutes.

3 Increase heat to high and pour in wine; cook 3 minutes.

4 Add remaining ingredients, including reserved tomato pulp, and bring to boil. Reduce heat to low and cook sauce 30 minutes. Do not cover. Stir occasionally.

5 Let sauce cool before refrigerating.

Fresh Tomato Sauté

¼ cup	olive oil	50 mL
3	shallots, peeled and chopped	3
3	garlic cloves, peeled, crushed and chopped	3
1 cup	dry white wine	250 mL
5	tomatoes, cored, peeled and seeded	5
1 tbsp	basil	15 mL
1 tsp	oregano	5 mL
¼ tsp	crushed chilies	1 mL
3 tbsp	chopped sun-dried tomatoes	45 mL
	salt and pepper	

1 Heat oil in sauté pan over medium heat. Add shallots and garlic; cook 3 minutes over low heat.

2 Add wine, increase heat to high, and cook 2 minutes.

3 Chop tomatoes and add to pan. Add seasonings and sun-dried tomatoes. Cook 10 minutes over high heat.

4 Reduce heat to low. Continue cooking mixture 5 to 8 minutes.

5 Cool before refrigerating.

Pesto Sauce

8	garlic cloves	8
2 cups	fresh basil leaves, washed and dried	500 mL
½ cup	grated Parmesan cheese	125 mL
½ cup	olive oil	125 mL
	salt and pepper	

1 Place unpeeled garlic cloves in saucepan with 1 cup (250 mL) water. Bring to boil and cook 4 minutes. Remove cloves from water and let cool. Peel cloves and place in food processor.

2 Add basil and cheese to garlic. Season well and blend several minutes until puréed.

3 While machine is blending, pour oil in thin stream through hole in top. Ingredients should be well incorporated.

4 To store pesto, transfer mixture to glass jar. Place piece of plastic wrap on surface of pesto and press down with fingers. Seal jar with tight-fitting lid. Sauce can be stored in refrigerator up to 3 days.

White Sauce

4 tbsp	butter	60 mL
1/2	onion, chopped	1/2
4 tbsp	flour	60 mL
2 cups	milk, heated	500 mL
	salt and white pepper	
	pinch of nutmeg	

1 Heat butter in saucepan over medium heat. Add onion and cook 2 minutes over low heat.

2 Stir in flour and continue cooking 1 minute.

3 Pour in milk, whisking constantly. Season well and add nutmeg. Cook sauce 8 to 10 minutes over low heat. Stir 3 to 4 times during cooking process.

4 Pass sauce through sieve into clean bowl. Cover with sheet of waxed paper, touching surface of sauce, and let cool before refrigerating.

5 This sauce will keep 2 to 3 days in refrigerator.

Spicy Gazpacho Sauce

1	celery stalk, diced	1
1	tomato, peeled, seeded and quartered	1
1	green bell pepper, diced	1
1	jalapeño pepper, seeded and chopped	1
2	shallots, peeled and chopped	2
2	garlic cloves, peeled	2
½ tsp	oregano	2 mL
1 cup	chicken stock, heated	250 mL
1 tbsp	cornstarch	15 mL
3 tbsp	cold water	45 mL
	salt and pepper	

1 Place celery, tomato, bell pepper, jalapeño pepper, shallots, garlic and oregano in food processor. Blend to incorporate.

2 Transfer mixture to saucepan. Pour in chicken stock and season well. Cook sauce 10 minutes over medium heat.

3 Dilute cornstarch in cold water. Stir into sauce and cook 1 minute over low heat to thicken. Transfer sauce to bowl and let cool before refrigerating.

4 Sauce can be stored in refrigerator for up to 3 days.

Rouille Pizza Spread

4	red bell peppers	4
7	garlic cloves, unpeeled	7
2 tbsp	white breadcrumbs	30 mL
½ cup	olive oil	125 mL
	salt and pepper	

1 Cut bell peppers in half and remove seeds. Oil skin and place cut-side-down on cookie sheet; broil 6 minutes in oven. Remove from oven and let cool. Peel off skin and set aside.

2 Place unpeeled garlic cloves in saucepan with 1 cup (250 mL) water. Bring to boil and cook 4 minutes. Remove cloves from water and let cool. Peel cloves and place in food processor.

3 Add bell peppers to food processor and blend with garlic until puréed. Add breadcrumbs and season well; blend again.

4 While machine is blending, pour oil in thin stream through hole in top. Ingredients should be well combined. Depending on consistency, add more oil if desired, up to ¼ cup (50 mL).

5 Correct seasoning, cover and keep refrigerated, up to 3 days, until ready to use.

Ratatouille Sauce

1	yellow bell pepper	1
1	red bell pepper	1
2 tbsp	olive oil	30 mL
1	onion, peeled and chopped	1
3	garlic cloves, peeled, crushed and chopped	3
2	shallots, peeled and chopped	2
1	medium eggplant, diced with skin	1
1	small zucchini, diced	1
4	tomatoes, peeled, seeded and chopped	4
2 tbsp	chopped fresh basil	30 mL
¼ tsp	thyme	1 mL
	salt and pepper	

1 Cut bell peppers in half and remove seeds. Oil skin and place cut-side-down on cookie sheet; broil 6 minutes in oven. Remove from oven and let cool. Peel off skin, slice thinly and set aside.

2 Heat oil in sauté pan over medium heat. Add onion, garlic and shallots; cook 4 minutes.

3 Add eggplant, season well and continue cooking 6 minutes. Add zucchini and cook 3 minutes.

4 Add remaining ingredients, mix well and cook 30 minutes over low heat. Stir occasionally.

5 Keep covered in refrigerator for up to 3 days, until ready to use.

Thick Pizza Sauce

4 tbsp	olive oil	60 mL
1	onion, peeled and chopped	1
3	garlic cloves, peeled, crushed and chopped	3
2	28 oz (796 mL) cans plum tomatoes	2
5 ½ oz	can tomato paste	156 mL
2 tbsp	chopped fresh basil	30 mL
1 tbsp	chopped fresh oregano	15 mL
1	chili pepper, seeded and chopped	1
½ tsp	thyme	2 mL
1	bay leaf	1
	salt and pepper	
	pinch of sugar	

1 Heat oil in large sauté pan over medium heat. Add onion and garlic; cook 3 minutes over low heat.

2 Chop tomatoes and add to pan with juice. Stir in tomato paste and remaining ingredients. Mix well.

3 Cook sauce, uncovered, 1 hour over low heat. Stir occasionally. Sauce should become thick.

4 Refrigerate for up to 3 days, until ready to use.

Tips on Making Pizza

●

Always bake pizza in a very hot oven and on the lower oven rack.
The simplest way is to use a solid or perforated pizza pan.

●

For a crisp crust, grease pizza pan with olive oil.

●

Supermarkets have a good selection of ready-made pizza dough
shells and ready-to-use pizza dough.

●

When making your own dough, be sure the water temperature is correct
and that you have a warm place for the dough to rise.

●

Rolling out pizza dough to just the right thickness takes some practice.
Rotate dough frequently and turn dough over during rolling to maintain
round shape. The final thickness of the dough is a matter of taste.
The thinner the crust, the crispier the pizza will be.

●

You may roll out pizza dough in different shapes other than circular:
square, rectangular, triangular, etc.

●

Always flute edges of pizza dough shell to prevent sauce from spilling
over. Spread sauce over pizza dough shell but not completely to edges.
Leave about a 1-in (2.5-cm) border.

●

The recipes give measurements for sauce and cheese. Depending on
your preference and the type of pizza dough shell used, you may
choose to decrease or increase the quantities suggested.

Basic Pizza Dough
two 14-in (36-cm) pizzas

1 ¼ cups	lukewarm water	300 mL
1	envelope yeast	1
3 ½ cups	all-purpose flour	875 mL
1 tsp	salt	5 mL
¼ cup	olive oil	50 mL
	pinch of sugar	

*It is important that water temperature be very close to 110°F (43°C).

1 Place ¼ cup (50 mL) lukewarm water in mixing bowl. Sprinkle yeast over water and let stand 2 minutes. Add pinch of sugar and cover bowl. Set aside in warm place for 5 to 6 minutes, until yeast starts to foam.

2 Place flour and salt in large mixing bowl. Make a well in center and pour in yeast. Add remaining water and oil; mix dough with fingers.

3 Once dough is well mixed gather into ball and place on floured work surface. Knead dough 10 minutes until smooth and elastic.

4 Shape into ball and place in oiled bowl. Cover with plastic wrap and let rise 2 hours in warm place.

5 Cut dough in half. Roll out each piece on floured work surface until desired thickness is reached. Rotate dough during rolling process to produce an even thickness and round shape.

6 Flute or crimp edges of crust. Garnish pizza and cook.

Vegetarian Pizza
14-in (36-cm) pizza

6	slices yellow summer squash	6
6	slices zucchini	6
5	slices red onion rings	5
1/2	green bell pepper, sliced	1/2
1/2	yellow bell pepper, sliced	1/2
4	slices Italian eggplant*	4
3 tbsp	olive oil	45 mL
3/4 cup	Thick Pizza Sauce (see p. 42)	175 mL
I	pizza dough shell	I
I cup	grated mozzarella cheese	250 mL
6	cherry tomatoes, halved	6
I	garlic clove, peeled and sliced	I
	salt and freshly ground pepper	

Preheat oven to 500°F (260°C).

1 Change oven setting to broil. Baste all vegetables, except cherry tomatoes, with oil. Place in roasting pan and broil 4 minutes. Season vegetables and set aside.

2 Set oven at original temperature.

3 Spread pizza sauce over pizza dough shell. Add broiled vegetables and cheese.

4 Arrange cherry tomatoes and sprinkle with garlic. Season well with pepper.

5 Cook 10 to 12 minutes in oven.

*Italian eggplant, often called baby eggplant, is much smaller than the regular variety and has a more delicate skin.

Zucchini Pizza
14-in (36-cm) pizza

3 tbsp	olive oil	45 mL
1	onion, peeled and chopped	1
2	garlic cloves, peeled, crushed and chopped	2
1	jalapeño pepper, seeded and chopped	1
1	zucchini, sliced ¼ in (5 mm) thick	1
2 tbsp	chopped fresh basil	30 mL
1 cup	Ratatouille Sauce (see p. 41)	250 mL
1	pizza dough shell	1
1¼ cups	grated mozzarella cheese	300 mL
	pinch of thyme	
	salt and freshly ground pepper	

Preheat oven to 500°F (260°C).

1 Heat oil in frying pan over medium heat. Add onion and cook 4 minutes. Add garlic, jalapeño pepper and zucchini. Add all seasonings, mix and cook 6 minutes over high heat.

2 Spread ratatouille sauce over pizza dough shell. Cover pizza with zucchini mixture and top with cheese. Season with pepper.

3 Cook 10 to 12 minutes in oven.

Focaccia Bread
(6 to 8 servings)

1 cup	lukewarm water	250 mL
½ tsp	sugar	2 mL
1	envelope yeast	1
2½ cups	unbleached white flour	625 mL
2 tbsp	butter	30 mL
½	onion, finely chopped	½
½ cup	chopped fresh basil	125 mL
4 tbsp	olive oil	60 mL
	salt	

1 Place water, sugar and yeast in mixing bowl. Set aside in warm place for 10 minutes.

2 Add three quarters of flour to yeast and mix to combine. When incorporated, set aside to rise in warm place for 2½ hours.

3 Heat butter in frying pan over medium heat. Add onion and cook 10 minutes over low heat. Add basil and continue cooking 2 minutes. Set aside.

4 Add remaining flour, pinch of salt and half of oil to dough. Mix well and add water if needed. Turn out onto floured work surface and knead 10 minutes.

5 Place dough in oiled bowl. Cover with plastic wrap and let rise another 2 hours in warm place.

6 Using a rolling pin, shape dough into rectangular shape, about 12 in x 16 in (30 x 40 cm). Slide onto cookie sheet and top with onion and basil garnish. Drizzle with remaining olive oil. Cook 14 to 18 minutes in oven preheated at 450°F (230°C). Serve warm.

Quattro Pizza Pie
14-in (36-cm) pizza

4	slices prosciutto	4
4 tbsp	olive oil	60 mL
12	fresh mushrooms, cleaned and sliced	12
¾ cup	Thick Pizza Sauce (see p. 42)	175 mL
1	pizza dough shell	1
8	slices mozzarella cheese	8
12	pitted black olives, sliced	12
4	artichoke hearts, marinated in oil, drained and quartered	4
	freshly ground pepper	

Preheat oven to 500°F (260°C).

1 Slice prosciutto into strips ½ in (1 cm) wide; set aside.

2 Heat 3 tbsp (45 mL) oil in frying pan over medium heat. Add mushrooms, season and cook 3 minutes. Set aside.

3 Spread pizza sauce over pizza dough shell. Cover with slices of mozzarella cheese.

4 Arrange olives, artichoke hearts, prosciutto and mushrooms separately on pizza, each ingredient covering one quarter of pizza pie.

5 Season with pepper and drizzle remaining oil over ingredients.

6 Cook 10 to 12 minutes in oven.

Pizza with Prosciutto, Tomato and Cheese
14-in (36-cm) pizza

¾ cup	Basic Fresh Tomato Sauce (see p. 35)	175 mL
1	pizza dough shell	1
3 oz	prosciutto, sliced in strips	90 g
1 cup	diced mozzarella cheese	250 mL
6	fresh basil leaves	6
2	garlic cloves, peeled and thinly sliced	2
2 tbsp	grated Parmesan cheese	30 mL
	freshly ground pepper	
	few drops of olive oil	

Preheat oven to 500°F (260°C).

1 Spread tomato sauce over pizza dough shell. Add prosciutto, mozzarella cheese and basil leaves.

2 Sprinkle garlic, then Parmesan over pizza. Season generously with pepper and sprinkle with a few drops of olive oil.

3 Cook 10 to 12 minutes in oven.

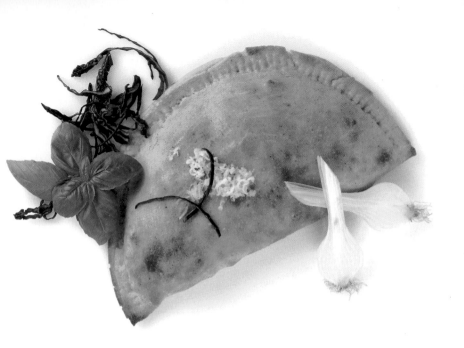

Super Stuffed Ground Beef Pizza
18-in (46-cm) pizza

3 tbsp	olive oil	45 mL
2	onions, peeled and sliced	2
2	garlic cloves, peeled, crushed and chopped	2
1	yellow bell pepper, sliced	1
3	anchovy fillets, drained and chopped	3
½ lb	lean ground beef	225 g
1	pizza dough shell*	1
⅓ lb	diced Caciocavallo cheese	150 g
	pinch of crushed chilies	
	salt and pepper	

Preheat oven to 450°F (230°C).

1 Heat 2 tbsp (30 mL) oil in frying pan over medium heat. Add onions, garlic and yellow pepper. Season and cook 8 minutes.

2 Add anchovies and ground beef; season and continue cooking 4 minutes. Stir in crushed chilies.

3 Brush *18-in (46-cm) pizza dough shell with oil. Spread filling on one half of dough. Add cheese and fold other side of dough over filling. Crimp edges shut.

4 Place dough on oiled cookie sheet. Brush exposed side of dough with oil. Cook 20 minutes in oven.

Pizza Stuffed with Spinach and Cheese
18-in (46-cm) pizza

1 ½ lb	fresh spinach, washed and trimmed	700 g
3 tbsp	butter	45 mL
2	garlic cloves, peeled, crushed and chopped	2
2 oz	chopped anchovies	60 g
¼ lb	ricotta cheese	125 g
1 tbsp	olive oil	15 mL
1	pizza dough shell*	1
3 oz	grated Gruyère cheese	90 g
	salt and pepper	

Preheat oven to 450°F (230°C).

1 Steam spinach for 3 minutes. Drain well and chop.

2 Heat butter in frying pan over medium heat. Add spinach and garlic; cook 3 minutes.

3 Transfer mixture to bowl. Add anchovies and ricotta cheese; mix well. Season with salt and pepper.

4 Brush oil over *18-in (46-cm) pizza dough shell. Spread spinach filling on one half of dough. Top with Gruyère cheese and season with pepper. Fold other side of dough over filling. Crimp edges shut.

5 Place dough on oiled cookie sheet. Brush exposed side of dough with oil. Cook 20 minutes in oven.

Pecorino Pizza with Pesto

14-in (36-cm) pizza

½ cup	Pesto Sauce (see p. 37)	125 mL
1	pizza dough shell	1
1 cup	grated mozzarella cheese	250 mL
2	large tomatoes, cored	2
2	garlic cloves, peeled and sliced	2
1	chili pepper, seeded and finely chopped	1
4	fresh basil leaves	4
½ cup	grated Pecorino cheese	125 mL
	salt and pepper	

Preheat oven to 500°F (260°C).

1 Spread pesto sauce over pizza dough shell. Cover with grated mozzarella cheese.

2 Slice tomatoes about ½ in (1 cm) thick and arrange on pizza. Season well and add garlic, chili pepper and basil leaves.

3 Top with Pecorino cheese.

4 Cook 10 to 12 minutes in oven.

Tex-Mex Pizza Pie
14-in (36-cm) pizza

2	yellow bell peppers	2
2/3 cup	grated mozzarella cheese	150 mL
1	pizza dough shell	1
2	tomatoes, sliced 1/3 in (8 mm) thick	2
1	jalapeño pepper, seeded and finely chopped	1
1	garlic clove, peeled, crushed and finely chopped	1
1 tbsp	chopped fresh basil	15 mL
1/2 cup	grated Pecorino Sardo cheese	125 mL
	freshly ground pepper	

Preheat oven to 500°F (260°C).

1 Cut bell peppers in half and remove seeds. Oil skin and place cut-side-down on cookie sheet; broil 6 minutes in oven. Remove from oven and let cool. Peel off skin, slice thinly and set aside.

2 Sprinkle mozzarella cheese over pizza dough shell. Arrange tomato slices on cheese.

3 Add yellow peppers and jalapeño pepper. Add garlic and basil. Top with Pecorino Sardo cheese and season well with pepper.

4 Cook 10 to 12 minutes in oven.

Pesto and Shrimp Pizza
14-in (36-cm) pizza

3 tbsp	olive oil	45 mL
½	zucchini, sliced	½
½ lb	shrimp, peeled and deveined	225 g
6	artichoke hearts, marinated in oil, drained and halved	6
½ cup	Pesto Sauce (see p. 37)	125 mL
1	pizza dough shell	1
1	tomato, sliced	1
1¼ cups	grated mozzarella cheese	300 mL
	salt and freshly ground pepper	

Preheat oven to 500°F (260°C).

1 Heat oil in frying pan over medium heat. Add zucchini and cook 2 minutes over high heat.

2 Add shrimp and artichoke hearts; season well. Continue cooking 2 minutes over high heat; set aside.

3 Spread pesto sauce over pizza dough shell. Arrange tomato slices and cover with cheese.

4 Cook 10 to 12 minutes in oven.

5 About 2 minutes before pizza is done, top with shrimp and vegetable mixture and season well with pepper. Complete cooking.

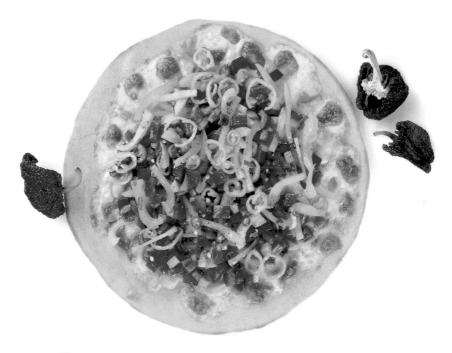

Sweet Pepper Pizza with Caciocavallo Cheese
14-in (36-cm) pizza

3	red bell peppers	3
2	yellow bell peppers	2
1	sweet banana pepper	1
4 tbsp	olive oil	60 mL
3	garlic cloves, peeled, crushed and chopped	3
1	chili pepper, seeded and finely chopped	1
2 tbsp	chopped fresh basil	30 mL
1	bay leaf	1
1	pizza dough shell	1
½ lb	diced Caciocavallo cheese	225 g
	freshly ground pepper	
	few drops of extra virgin olive oil	

1 Cut bell peppers and banana pepper in half and remove seeds. Oil skin and place cut-side-down on cookie sheet; broil 18 minutes in oven. Turn peppers over once during cooking. Remove from oven and place in large bowl. Cover bowl with plastic wrap. Let peppers steam 3 minutes. Peel and discard skins. Slice peppers.

2 Transfer sliced peppers to clean bowl. Add oil, garlic, chili pepper, basil and bay leaf. Season with pepper. Marinate 2 hours. Remove bay leaf.

3 Preheat oven to 500°F (260°C).

4 Brush extra virgin olive oil over pizza dough shell. Add cheese and top with marinated peppers.

5 Cook 10 to 12 minutes in oven.

Meat, Onion and Bell Pepper Pizza
14-in (36-cm) pizza

3 tbsp	olive oil	45 mL
1/2	red onion, chopped	1/2
2	garlic cloves, peeled, crushed and chopped	2
1/2	red bell pepper, thinly sliced	1/2
3	Italian sausages, meat removed from casings	3
3/4 cup	Thick Pizza Sauce (see p. 42)	175 mL
1	pizza dough shell	1
1 tbsp	chopped fresh basil	15 mL
1 tsp	oregano	5 mL
1 cup	grated mozzarella cheese	250 mL
	salt and pepper	
	few drops of extra virgin olive oil	

Preheat oven to 500°F (260°C).

1 Heat oil in frying pan over medium heat. Add onion, garlic and red pepper; season well. Cook 3 minutes.

2 Add sausage meat and continue cooking 4 minutes.

3 Spread pizza sauce over pizza dough shell. Cover with sausage mixture and sprinkle seasonings over meat. Top with cheese.

4 Cook 10 to 12 minutes in oven. Drizzle extra virgin olive oil over pizza just before serving.

Mexican Pizza with Monterey Jack
14-in (36-cm) pizza

4 tbsp	olive oil	60 mL
1/2	onion, chopped	1/2
2	green onions, chopped	2
2	garlic cloves, peeled, crushed and chopped	2
I	tomato, peeled, seeded and diced	I
1/4 tsp	crushed chilies	I mL
3/4 cup	Spicy Gazpacho Sauce (see p. 39)	175 mL
I	pizza dough shell	I
I cup	grated Monterey Jack cheese	250 mL
3/4 cup	grated Parmesan cheese	175 mL
	salt and pepper	

Preheat oven to 500°F (260°C).

1 Heat half of oil in frying pan over medium heat. Add onions, garlic, tomato and crushed chilies. Season well and cook 6 minutes.

2 Spread gazpacho sauce over pizza dough shell. Top with onion/tomato mixture and cover with both cheeses. Drizzle remaining olive oil over ingredients and season well.

3 Cook 10 to 12 minutes in oven.

Spicy Tomato and Cheese Pizza
14-in (36-cm) pizza

I	small eggplant	I
4 tbsp	olive oil	60 mL
½ cup	Ratatouille Sauce (see p. 41)	125 mL
I	pizza dough shell	I
I	dried chili pepper, crushed	I
¼ cup	Thick Pizza Sauce (see p. 42)	50 mL
2	garlic cloves, peeled and sliced	2
I ¼ cups	grated mozzarella cheese	300 mL
	coarse salt	
	freshly ground pepper	
	few drops extra virgin olive oil	

Preheat oven to 500°F (260°C).

1 Cut eggplant into 10 slices, about ¼ in (5 mm) thick. Spread slices on paper towel and sprinkle with coarse salt. Let stand 30 minutes. Drain and pat dry.

2 Heat oil in frying pan over medium heat. Add eggplant slices and cook 3 minutes on each side. Remove and set aside.

3 Spread ratatouille sauce over pizza dough shell. Mix dried chili pepper with pizza sauce; spread over pizza.

4 Sprinkle garlic over pizza and cover with cheese. Arrange eggplant slices and season well with pepper. Drizzle few drops of extra virgin olive oil over ingredients.

5 Cook 10 to 12 minutes in oven.

Double Tomato Eggplant Pizza
14-in (36-cm) pizza

4 tbsp	olive oil	60 mL
1	small eggplant, sliced ¼ in (5 mm) thick	1
1	large onion, peeled and finely chopped	1
¾ cup	Basic Fresh Tomato Sauce (see p. 35)	175 mL
1	pizza dough shell	1
12	slices Fontina cheese	12
½ cup	sun-dried tomatoes	125 mL
	freshly ground pepper	

Preheat oven to 500°F (260°C).

1 Heat 3 tbsp (45 mL) oil in frying pan over high heat. Add eggplant slices and cook 3 minutes on each side. When cooked, remove from pan and set aside.

2 Add remaining oil to hot frying pan. Add onion and reduce heat to medium; cook 6 minutes.

3 Spread tomato sauce over pizza dough shell. Arrange eggplant slices and onion over sauce. Season well with pepper. Cover with slices of cheese and top with sun-dried tomatoes.

4 Cook 10 to 12 minutes in oven.

Pizza Sandwich alla Ricotta

14-in (36-cm) pizza

5 tbsp	Thick Pizza Sauce (see p. 42)	75 mL
1	pizza dough shell	1
½ lb	ricotta cheese	225 g
3 oz	mortadella sausage, thinly sliced	90 g
2	hard-boiled eggs, sliced	2
	few drops olive oil	

Preheat oven to 450°F (230°C).

1 Spread pizza sauce over pizza dough shell. It is especially important in this recipe to leave a ½-in (1-cm) border free of sauce.

2 Arrange cheese, sausage and eggs over pizza. Sprinkle with few drops of oil.

3 Wet edges of dough with cold water. Carefully fold dough in half. Press edges of dough together, forming seal.

4 Cook 20 minutes in oven.

Ham and Sausage Pizza with Chutney
14-in (36-cm) pizza

2 tbsp	olive oil	30 mL
¾ cup	cooked ham, cut in strips	175 mL
¾ cup	mortadella sausage, cut in strips	175 mL
6 tbsp	chutney	90 mL
1 cup	Ratatouille Sauce (see p. 41)	250 mL
1	pizza dough shell	1
10	slices Scamorze cheese	10
½ cup	pitted Kalamata olives, chopped	125 mL
	freshly ground pepper	
	few drops of extra virgin olive oil	

Preheat oven to 500°F (260°C).

1 Heat olive oil in frying pan over medium heat. Add ham and sausage; cook 2 minutes. Stir in chutney and continue cooking 1 minute. Set aside.

2 Spread ratatouille sauce over pizza dough shell. Add ham and sausage mixture and cover with slices of cheese. Season with pepper.

3 Top with chopped olives and drizzle a few drops of extra virgin olive oil over ingredients.

4 Cook 10 to 12 minutes in oven.

Asparagus Pizza with Scamorze
14-in (36-cm) pizza

2	bunches fresh asparagus	2
2 tbsp	butter	30 mL
1	yellow bell pepper, chopped	1
1 cup	White Sauce, heated (see p. 38)	250 mL
1	pizza dough shell	1
¾ cup	grated Scamorze cheese	175 mL
½ cup	sliced pitted black olives	125 mL
¾ cup	grated Gruyère cheese	175 mL
	salt and pepper	
	cayenne pepper to taste	

Preheat oven to 500°F (260°C).

1 Pare asparagus if necessary and trim stem ends. Soak briefly in cold water, then cut stalks into 1-in (2.5-cm) pieces. Steam just until tender.

2 Heat butter in frying pan over medium heat. Add asparagus and chopped bell pepper. Cook 3 minutes.

3 Spread white sauce over pizza dough shell. Add Scamorze cheese and top with hot vegetables; season well. Add olives and cover with Gruyère cheese. Season with black pepper and cayenne pepper to taste.

4 Cook 10 to 12 minutes in oven.

Hawaiian Pizza
14-in (36-cm) pizza

³/₄ cup	Basic Fresh Tomato Sauce (see p. 35)	175 mL
1	pizza dough shell	1
1 cup	sliced cooked mushrooms	250 mL
2 cups	cooked diced lobster meat	500 mL
1 ¼ cups	grated mozzarella cheese	300 mL
1 cup	diced pineapple	250 mL
	salt and pepper	
	paprika to taste	

Preheat oven to 500°F (260°C).

1 Spread tomato sauce over pizza dough shell. Top with mushrooms and lobster meat and cover with cheese. Season with salt and pepper.

2 Top with diced pineapple. Season with paprika to taste.

3 Cook 10 to 12 minutes in oven.

Cheese Lover's Pizza
14-in (36-cm) pizza

½ cup	Pesto Sauce (see p. 37)	125 mL
1	pizza dough shell	1
2	large tomatoes, cored	2
2	garlic cloves, peeled and thinly sliced	2
½ lb	Bel Paese cheese, diced	225 g
	freshly ground pepper	
	extra virgin olive oil	

Preheat oven to 500°F (260°C).

1 Spread pesto sauce over pizza dough shell. Slice tomatoes about ¼ in (5 mm) thick and arrange on pizza.

2 Scatter sliced garlic over pizza and season with pepper. Top with diced cheese and drizzle ingredients with a few drops of extra virgin olive oil.

3 Cook 10 to 12 minutes in oven.

Pizza à la Rouille
14-in (36-cm) pizza

1 1/2	green bell peppers	1 1/2
1	pizza dough shell	1
1/2 cup	Rouille Pizza Spread (see p. 40)	125 mL
3/4 cup	grated Pecorino cheese	175 mL
3/4 cup	Fresh Tomato Sauté (see p. 36)	175 mL
1 tbsp	olive oil	15 mL
	freshly ground pepper	

Preheat oven to 500°F (260°C).

1 Cut bell peppers in half and remove seeds. Oil skin and place cut-side-down on cookie sheet; broil 6 minutes in oven. Remove from oven and let cool. Peel off skin, slice and set aside.

2 Cover pizza dough shell with thin layer of Rouille Pizza Spread.

3 Arrange cheese, sliced green pepper and Fresh Tomato Sauté over sauce.

4 Drizzle olive oil over ingredients and season with pepper.

5 Cook 10 to 12 minutes in oven.

Tasty Clam Pizza
14-in (36-cm) pizza

1 tbsp	olive oil	15 mL
1	pizza dough shell	1
2	garlic cloves, peeled and thinly sliced	2
¾ cup	Basic Fresh Tomato Sauce (see p. 35)	175 mL
10	slices Provolone cheese	10
¾ cup	canned clams, drained	175 mL
3 tbsp	grated Parmesan cheese	45 mL
	freshly ground pepper	

Preheat oven to 500°F (260°C).

1 Brush oil over pizza dough shell and add garlic. Spread tomato sauce over pizza and top with Provolone cheese. Season well with pepper.

2 Cook 10 to 12 minutes in oven.

3 About 4 minutes before pizza is done, add clams and Parmesan cheese. Complete cooking.

Pizza with Fresh Oyster Mushrooms
14-in (36-cm) pizza

3 tbsp	olive oil	45 mL
1	large red onion, peeled and cut in rings	1
4	large tomatoes, peeled, seeded and coarsely chopped	4
30 mL	butter	2 tbsp
8	fresh oyster mushrooms, thickly sliced	8
1	pizza dough shell	1
1 cup	grated Monterey Jack cheese	250 mL
½ cup	diced leftover cooked chicken	125 mL
	salt and pepper	

Preheat oven to 500°F (260°C).

1 Heat oil in sauté pan over medium heat. Add onion and cook 8 minutes. Add tomatoes, season and continue cooking 15 minutes.

2 Heat butter in small frying pan over medium heat. Add oyster mushrooms and sauté 2 to 3 minutes.

3 Spread tomato mixture over pizza dough shell. Add mushrooms and top with grated cheese. Season with pepper.

4 Cook 10 to 12 minutes in oven.

5 About 4 minutes before pizza is done, add chopped chicken and complete cooking.

Onion Pizza with Gorgonzola Cheese
14-in (36-cm) pizza
(or 4 individual-size pizzas)

¼ cup	olive oil	50 mL
2	large onions, peeled and thinly sliced	2
1	pizza dough shell	1
½ cup	pine nuts	125 mL
¾ lb	crumbled Gorgonzola cheese	350 g
12	fresh basil leaves	12
	salt and freshly ground pepper	

Preheat oven to 500°F (260°C).

1 Heat 3 tbsp (45 mL) oil in frying pan over medium heat. Add onions, season and cook 15 minutes. Reduce heat if onions brown too quickly.

2 Cover bottom of pizza dough shell with cooked onions. Add pine nuts and top with cheese. Arrange basil leaves and drizzle remaining oil over ingredients. Season with pepper.

3 Cook 10 to 12 minutes in oven.

Fennel and Leek Pizza
14-in (36-cm) pizza

2	small leeks, white part only	2
1	small fennel bulb	1
3 tbsp	olive oil	45 mL
1	shallot, peeled and chopped	1
1	pizza dough shell	1
½ cup	Rouille Pizza Spread (see p. 40)	125 mL
1¼ cups	grated Fontina cheese	300 mL
½ cup	sliced green pitted olives	125 mL
4 tbsp	grated Parmesan cheese	60 mL
	salt and pepper	

Preheat oven to 500°F (260°C).

1 Slit leeks from top to bottom twice, leaving 1 in (2.5 cm) intact at base. Wash leeks under cold, running water to remove grit and sand. Drain and slice thinly.

2 Peel fennel and slice thinly. Heat oil in frying pan over medium heat. Add fennel, leeks and shallot. Season, cover and cook 18 minutes over low heat. Stir occasionally to prevent sticking.

3 Cover pizza dough shell with rouille spread. Add cooked fennel and leeks.

4 Cover pizza with Fontina cheese. Top with olives and Parmesan cheese. Season well with pepper.

5 Cook 10 to 12 minutes in oven.

Pizza with Sautéed Chicken and Fontina
14-in (36-cm) pizza

3 tbsp	olive oil	45 mL
1	whole skinned boneless chicken breast, thinly sliced	1
2	shallots, peeled and chopped	2
2	green onions, chopped	2
1 tbsp	chopped fresh basil	15 mL
1 tsp	herbes de Provence	5 mL
1/4 cup	pine nuts	50 mL
3/4 cup	Thick Pizza Sauce (see p. 42)	175 mL
1	pizza dough shell	1
1 cup	diced Fontina cheese	250 mL
	salt and pepper	

Preheat oven to 500°F (260°C).

1 Heat oil in frying pan over medium heat. Add chicken strips, season and cook 2 minutes on each side. Add shallots, green onions, seasonings and pine nuts. Continue cooking 1 minute, then set aside.

2 Spread pizza sauce over pizza dough shell. Add chicken mixture and top with cheese. Season well with pepper.

3 Cook 10 to 12 minutes in oven.

Pizza with Cooked Garlic and Japanese Eggplant
14-in (36-cm) pizza

4 tbsp	olive oil	60 mL
I	garlic bulb, separated into cloves	I
I	Japanese ("baby") eggplant	I
¾ cup	Thick Pizza Sauce (see p. 42)	175 mL
I	pizza dough shell	I
1½ cups	grated Fontina cheese	375 mL
3 tbsp	chopped fresh basil	45 mL
	freshly ground pepper	
	few drops extra virgin olive oil	

Preheat oven to 400°F (200°C).

1 Heat 3 tbsp (45 mL) oil in frying pan over medium heat. Add garlic cloves (do not peel) and cook 15 minutes. Reduce heat if necessary to prevent burning. Remove, let cool and peel cloves.

2 Increase oven temperature to 500°F (260°C).

3 Meanwhile, cut eggplant into slices about 1/4 in (5 mm) thick. Brush both sides with 1 tbsp (15 mL) oil. Cook 12 minutes in oven, turning slices over once.

4 Spread pizza sauce over pizza dough shell. Cover with cheese and top with eggplant slices and garlic cloves.

5 Season with pepper. Sprinkle with basil and a few drops of extra virgin olive oil.

6 Cook 10 to 12 minutes in oven.

Artichoke and Eggplant Sauce Pizza
14-in (36-cm) pizza

3 tbsp	olive oil	45 mL
3	onions, peeled and thinly sliced	3
1 cup	Ratatouille Sauce (see p. 41)	250 mL
1	pizza dough shell	1
8	artichoke hearts, marinated in oil, drained and quartered	8
1 tbsp	chopped fresh basil	15 mL
3 tbsp	grated Parmesan cheese	45 mL
1 ½ cups	grated Fontina cheese	375 mL
	freshly ground pepper	

Preheat oven to 500°F (260°C).

1 Heat oil in frying pan over medium heat. Add onions and cook 15 minutes over low heat. Do not let onions burn.

2 Spread ratatouille sauce over pizza dough shell. Add onions, artichoke hearts and basil.

3 Top with grated cheeses and season well with pepper.

4 Cook 10 to 12 minutes in oven.

Cajun Chicken Pizza
14-in (36-cm) pizza

3 tbsp	butter	45 mL
1/2	small onion, chopped	1/2
1/2	celery stalk, diced	1/2
I	bell pepper, sliced	I
I	whole skinned boneless chicken breast	I
1/2 tsp	oregano	2 mL
3/4 cup	Basic Fresh Tomato Sauce (see p. 35)	175 mL
I	pizza dough shell	I
I tbsp	chopped fresh basil	15 mL
I 1/4 cups	grated smoked mozzarella cheese	300 mL
	pinch of cayenne pepper	
	pinch of thyme	
	salt and white pepper	

Preheat oven to 500°F (260°C).

1 Heat butter in sauté pan over medium heat. Add onion, celery and bell pepper; cook 2 minutes.

2 Split chicken breast into two. Add to vegetables in pan and cook 2 minutes on each side. Add oregano, cayenne pepper, thyme, salt and pepper. Mix well and cover pan. Cook chicken 10 to 12 minutes over low heat. Set pan aside.

3 Spread tomato sauce over pizza dough shell. Add chopped basil and grated cheese. Place pizza in oven and cook 8 minutes.

4 Remove pizza from oven. Slice chicken breasts and arrange on pizza. Top with chopped vegetables and resume cooking for 3 to 4 minutes.

Greek Pizza Pie
14-in (36-cm) pizza

I	medium eggplant	I
¼ cup	olive oil	50 mL
I	pizza dough shell	I
I cup	Fresh Tomato Sauté (see p. 36)	250 mL
½ cup	feta cheese, crumbled	125 mL
¼ cup	sliced pitted black olives	50 mL
	freshly ground pepper	

Preheat oven to 500°F (260°C).

1 Cut eggplant into 12 round slices. Heat 3 tbsp (45 mL) oil in frying pan over medium heat. Cook eggplant slices 2 minutes on each side over high heat; set aside.

2 Brush dough with remaining olive oil. Spread sautéed tomatoes over dough and add cheese.

3 Arrange eggplant slices on pizza and top with sliced olives. Season with pepper.

4 Cook 10 to 12 minutes in oven.

Red Salsa Pizza with Pepperoni
14-in (36-cm) pizza

1	large red bell pepper	1
2	green bell peppers	2
1 cup	wine vinegar	250 mL
3 tbsp	sugar	45 mL
2	tomatoes, peeled, seeded and chopped	2
2	green onions, chopped	2
2	garlic cloves, peeled, crushed and chopped	2
1	jalapeño pepper, seeded and chopped	1
1	pizza dough shell	1
1¼ cups	grated mozzarella cheese	300 mL
15	slices pepperoni	15
½ cup	chopped pitted black olives	125 mL
	salt and pepper	
	few drops extra virgin olive oil	

Preheat oven to 500°F (260°C).

1 Cut bell peppers in half and remove seeds. Oil skin and place cut-side-down on cookie sheet; broil 8 minutes in oven. Remove from oven and place in large bowl. Cover bowl with plastic wrap. Let peppers steam 3 minutes. Peel and discard skins. Dice peppers and place in mixing bowl; set aside.

2 Place vinegar and sugar in small saucepan. Cook until liquid becomes golden in color. Pour over diced peppers in mixing bowl.

3 Add tomatoes, green onions, garlic and jalapeño pepper; mix and season well. Marinate 5 minutes.

4 Spread salsa over pizza dough shell. Add cheese and pepperoni. Top with chopped olives. Sprinkle with a few drops of extra virgin olive oil.

5 Cook 10 to 12 minutes in oven.

Garden Fresh Pizza
14-in (36-cm) pizza

1	small bunch fresh asparagus	1
1	small head broccoli	1
3 tbsp	olive oil	45 mL
1	large carrot, pared and thinly sliced	1
2	garlic cloves, peeled, crushed and chopped	2
1 cup	White Sauce, heated (see p. 38)	250 mL
1	pizza dough shell	1
1½ cups	grated Gruyère cheese	375 mL
	salt and pepper	
	pinch of paprika	
	few drops of extra virgin olive oil	

Preheat oven to 500°F (260°C).

1 Pare asparagus if necessary and trim stem ends. Soak briefly in cold water, then cut stalks into 1-in (2.5-cm) pieces. Divide broccoli into small florets.

2 Heat oil in frying pan over medium heat. Add asparagus, broccoli, carrot and garlic. Season, cover and cook 6 to 8 minutes over low heat.

3 Spread white sauce over pizza dough shell. Add cooked vegetables and top with cheese. Season well and sprinkle with paprika. Drizzle a few drops of extra virgin olive oil over ingredients.

4 Cook 10 to 12 minutes in oven.

Black Olive Pizza with Pecorino Cheese
14-in (36-cm) pizza

3 tbsp	olive oil	45 mL
1	onion, peeled and finely chopped	1
³/₄ cup	Basic Fresh Tomato Sauce (see p. 35)	175 mL
1	pizza dough shell	1
2	garlic cloves, peeled and thinly sliced	2
¹/₂ cup	grated Pecorino cheese	125 mL
¹/₃ cup	pitted black olives, sliced	75 mL
	freshly ground pepper	

Preheat oven to 500°F (260°C).

1 Heat half of oil in frying pan over medium heat. Add chopped onion and cook 5 minutes over low heat.

2 Spread tomato sauce over pizza dough shell. Sprinkle cooked onion and garlic over sauce.

3 Add cheese, then black olives. Drizzle remaining oil over ingredients and season with pepper.

4 Cook 10 to 12 minutes in oven.

Artichoke Pizza
14-in (36-cm) pizza

3 tbsp	butter	45 mL
1	shallot, peeled and chopped	1
10	fresh mushrooms, cleaned and sliced	10
¾ cup	Thick Pizza Sauce (see p. 42)	175 mL
1	pizza dough shell	1
⅔ cup	grated mozzarella cheese	150 mL
2 oz	prosciutto, sliced	60 g
8	artichoke hearts, marinated in oil	8
¼ cup	sliced pitted black olives	50 mL
1 tbsp	olive oil	15 mL
1 tbsp	chopped fresh basil	15 mL
	salt and freshly ground pepper	

Preheat oven to 500°F (260°C).

1 Heat butter in frying pan over medium heat. Add shallot and mushrooms; season well. Cook 4 minutes.

2 Spread pizza sauce over pizza dough shell. Arrange cooked mushrooms over sauce. Add cheese and prosciutto.

3 Drain artichoke hearts, slice in half and place on pizza with black olives. Drizzle oil over ingredients and sprinkle with basil.

4 Cook 10 to 12 minutes in oven.

Pizza Provençale
two 14-in (36-cm) pizzas

½ cup	olive oil	125 mL
10	onions, peeled and finely chopped	10
3	garlic cloves, peeled	3
3	sprigs fresh parsley	3
½ tsp	thyme	2 mL
2	pizza dough shells	2
18	anchovy fillets	18
24	pitted black olives, halved	24
	freshly ground pepper	
	grated Parmesan cheese to taste	

Preheat oven to 500°F (260°C).

1 Heat oil in frying pan over medium heat. Add onions, whole garlic cloves, parsley and thyme. Season with pepper and cook 20 minutes over medium heat. Onions should become golden in color, but not brown.

2 When cooked, discard garlic and parsley sprigs. Spread onions over pizza dough shells.

3 Drain anchovy fillets and rinse under cold water. Drain again and pat dry with paper towels. Arrange fillets on pizzas.

4 Top with black olives and grated Parmesan cheese to taste.

5 Cook 10 to 12 minutes in oven.

Pesto Pizza with Sun-Dried Tomatoes
14-in (36-cm) pizza
(or 4 individual-size pizzas)

2 tbsp	cornmeal	30 mL
1	pizza dough shell	1
½ cup	Pesto Sauce (see p. 37)	125 mL
1¼ cups	grated mozzarella cheese	300 mL
4 tbsp	chopped sun-dried tomatoes	60 mL
¼ cup	pine nuts	50 mL
	freshly ground pepper	
	few drops of olive oil	

Preheat oven to 500°F (260°C).

1 Line oiled pizza pan with cornmeal and position pizza dough shell.

2 Spread pesto sauce over pizza. Add cheese, sun-dried tomatoes and pine nuts. Season well with pepper. Drizzle a few drops of oil over ingredients.

3 Cook 10 to 12 minutes in oven.

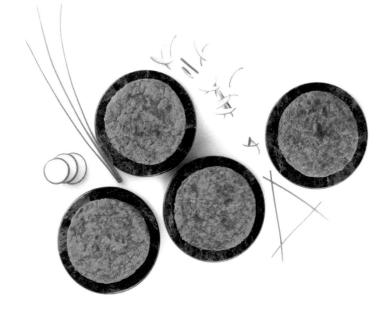

Party Pizza Muffins
(8 servings)

2 cups	grated Pecorino Sardo cheese	500 mL
I cup	grated cheddar cheese	250 mL
I ½ cups	Thick Pizza Sauce (see p. 42)	375 mL
2 tbsp	chopped fresh basil	30 mL
3	garlic cloves, peeled, crushed and chopped	3
I	jalapeño pepper, seeded and chopped	I
8	English muffins, split in half	8
	salt and pepper	

Preheat oven to 450°F (230°C).

1 Place all ingredients, except muffins, in food processor. Blend several seconds until combined.

2 Arrange split English muffins on cookie sheets. Top each with pizza mixture and cook 10 to 12 minutes in oven.

Tasty Sausage Pizza
14-in (36-cm) pizza

3 tbsp	olive oil	45 mL
¹⁄₃ lb	Italian sausage, sliced	150 g
¹⁄₂	green bell pepper, thinly sliced	¹⁄₂
2 oz	sliced pimiento pepper	60 g
1	onion, peeled and thinly sliced	1
¹⁄₄ tsp	crushed chilies	1 mL
1	pizza dough shell	1
³⁄₄ cup	Thick Pizza Sauce (see p. 42)	175 mL
1 ¹⁄₄ cups	grated mozzarella cheese	300 mL
4 tbsp	grated Romano cheese	60 mL
	salt and pepper	

Preheat oven to 500°F (260°C).

1 Heat 2 tbsp (30 mL) oil in frying pan over medium heat. Add sausage, green pepper, pimiento, onion, and crushed chilies. Season well and cook 4 minutes.

2 Spread sausage mixture over pizza dough shell. Cover with pizza sauce and top with mozzarella and Romano cheeses. Season well with pepper and drizzle remaining oil over ingredients.

3 Cook 10 to 12 minutes in oven.

Cocktail Party Pizza
14-in (36-cm) pizza

2	apples	2
6 oz	Brie cheese, chilled	170 g
1	pizza dough shell	1
2 oz	blue cheese, crumbled	60 g
	few drops of lemon juice	
	few drops of olive oil	
	freshly ground pepper	

Preheat oven to 500°F (260°C).

1 Core, peel and slice apples. Place in bowl and toss with lemon juice to prevent discoloring.

2 Remove rind from Brie cheese and discard. Cut cheese into small pieces.

3 Arrange sliced apples in a circle pattern on pizza dough shell. Top with pieces of Brie and crumbled blue cheese.

4 Drizzle olive oil over cheese and season well with pepper.

5 Cook a maximum of 10 minutes in oven.

Sliced Tomato Pizza with Provolone
14-in (36-cm) pizza

2 tbsp	olive oil	30 mL
I	pizza dough shell	I
2	tomatoes, cored, peeled and thickly sliced	2
2	garlic cloves, peeled and thinly sliced	2
2 tbsp	chopped fresh basil	30 mL
I tsp	oregano	5 mL
½ cup	grated Provolone cheese	125 mL
¾ cup	grated mozzarella cheese	175 mL
4	slices crisp cooked bacon, chopped	4
	salt and freshly ground pepper	

Preheat oven to 500°F (260°C).

1 Brush olive oil over pizza dough shell.

2 Arrange tomato slices on pizza. Add garlic, basil and oregano. Season well.

3 Add grated Provolone cheese and pepper. Add mozzarella cheese.

4 Cook 10 to 12 minutes in oven.

5 About 3 minutes before pizza is done, add chopped bacon and complete cooking.

Bocconcini Pizza
14-in (36-cm) pizza

1 cup	Thick Pizza Sauce (see p. 42)	250 mL
1	pizza dough shell	1
³/₄ cup	diced Bocconcini cheese	175 mL
¹/₂ cup	fresh basil leaves	125 mL
¹/₂ tsp	oregano	2 mL
3 tbsp	olive oil	45 mL
	freshly ground pepper	

Preheat oven to 500°F (260°C).

1 Spread pizza sauce over pizza dough shell.

2 Arrange cheese, basil leaves and oregano over pizza. Drizzle olive oil over ingredients and season generously with pepper.

3 Cook 10 to 12 minutes in oven.

Ratatouille Pizza with Pepperoni and Mushrooms
14-in (36-cm) pizza

1	small chili pepper, seeded and chopped	1
1 cup	Ratatouille Sauce (see p. 41)	250 mL
1	pizza dough shell	1
¾ cup	grated mozzarella cheese	175 mL
15	slices pepperoni	15
6	fresh mushrooms, cleaned and sliced	6
6	fresh basil leaves	6
2 tbsp	olive oil	30 mL
	freshly ground pepper	

Preheat oven to 500°F (260°C).

1 Mix chopped chili pepper with ratatouille sauce. Spread over pizza dough shell.

2 Add cheese, pepperoni, mushrooms and basil leaves. Drizzle oil over ingredients and season with pepper.

3 Cook 10 to 12 minutes in oven.

Shallot Pizza with Kalamata Olives
14-in (36-cm) pizza

4 tbsp	olive oil	60 mL
2 lb	shallots, peeled	900 g
1 tbsp	brown sugar	15 mL
½ lb	fresh mushrooms, cleaned and sliced	225 g
1	pizza dough shell	1
¼ lb	prosciutto, sliced ½ in (1 cm) wide	125 g
1	garlic clove, peeled and sliced	1
1¼ cups	grated Fontina cheese	300 mL
½ cup	pitted Kalamata olives, halved	125 mL
4	anchovy fillets, drained and chopped	4
	salt and pepper	
	extra virgin olive oil	

Preheat oven to 500°F (260°C).

1 Heat 3 tbsp (45 mL) oil in sauté pan over medium heat. Add shallots and season; cook 30 minutes over low heat.

2 Add brown sugar, mix and cook 3 minutes. Remove shallots from pan and set aside.

3 Add remaining oil to hot pan. Cook mushrooms 3 minutes over high heat.

4 Arrange shallots over pizza dough shell. Add mushrooms and season with pepper. Add prosciutto and garlic. Cover with cheese.

5 Top with olives and anchovies. Sprinkle ingredients with extra virgin olive oil.

6 Cook 10 to 12 minutes in oven.

Shrimp Pizza with Purée of Sweet Peppers
14-in (36-cm) pizza

3	red bell peppers	3
2	green bell peppers	2
1	yellow bell pepper	1
6	garlic cloves, unpeeled	6
1/4 cup	Thick Pizza Sauce (see p. 42)	50 mL
1	pizza dough shell	1
1 1/4 cups	grated Fontina cheese	300 mL
1/2 lb	fresh shrimp, peeled and deveined	225 g
1/2 cup	pitted black olives, sliced	125 mL
1 tbsp	chopped fresh basil	15 mL
	freshly ground pepper	
	few drops of olive oil	

Preheat oven to 500°F (260°C).

1 Cut bell peppers in half and remove seeds. Oil skin and place cut-side-down on cookie sheet; broil 15 to 18 minutes in oven. Turn peppers over once during cooking. Remove from oven and place in large bowl. Cover bowl with plastic wrap. Let peppers steam 3 minutes. Peel and discard skins.

2 Place unpeeled garlic cloves in saucepan with 1 cup (250 mL) water. Bring to boil and cook 4 minutes. Remove cloves from water and let cool. Peel and purée flesh.

3 Place peppers in food processor with garlic. Blend together for several seconds. Add pizza sauce, season and blend to incorporate.

4 Spread bell pepper mixture over pizza dough shell. Top with cheese and cook 6 minutes in oven.

5 Slice shrimp in half and arrange on pizza. Add olives and basil; season well with pepper. Continue cooking for 4 to 6 minutes.

6 Sprinkle with a few drops of olive oil before serving.

Pizza à la Crème
14-in (36-cm) pizza

3 tbsp	olive oil	45 mL
¾ lb	fresh mushrooms, cleaned and sliced	350 g
2	shallots, peeled and chopped	2
1 cup	White Sauce, heated (see p. 38)	250 mL
1	pizza dough shell	1
1¼ cups	grated mozzarella cheese	300 mL
3	slices crisp cooked bacon, chopped	3
	salt and pepper	
	paprika to taste	

Preheat oven to 500°F (260°C).

1 Heat oil in frying pan over medium heat. Add mushrooms and shallots. Season and cook 5 minutes over high heat. Remove and set aside.

2 Spread white sauce over pizza dough shell. Cover with mushrooms and top with cheese. Season generously with pepper and paprika to taste.

3 Cook 10 to 12 minutes in oven.

4 About 2 minutes before pizza is done, add chopped bacon and complete cooking.

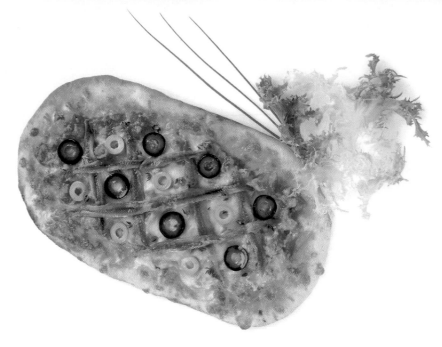

Double Olive Tomato Pizza
14-in (36-cm) pizza

15	anchovy fillets, drained	15
3 tbsp	milk	45 mL
2 tbsp	olive oil	30 mL
3	tomatoes, peeled, seeded and chopped	3
2	garlic cloves, peeled, crushed and chopped	2
1 tbsp	chopped fresh basil	15 mL
1/4 tsp	thyme	1 mL
1/4 tsp	oregano	1 mL
1	pizza dough shell	1
1 1/2 cups	grated mozzarella cheese	375 mL
1/4 cup	green pitted olives, sliced	50 mL
1/4 cup	black pitted olives, sliced	50 mL
	freshly ground pepper	

Preheat oven to 500°F (260°C).

1 Soak anchovy fillets in milk for 3 minutes. Remove and set aside to drain on paper towel.

2 Heat oil in frying pan over medium heat. Add tomatoes, garlic and seasonings. Cook 8 minutes.

3 Spread hot tomato mixture over pizza dough shell. Cover with cheese and add green olives.

4 Arrange anchovy fillets in lattice pattern and decorate with black olives. Season with pepper.

5 Cook 10 to 12 minutes in oven.

Leek and Ham Pizza
14-in (36-cm) pizza

4	leeks, white part only	4
3 tbsp	olive oil	45 mL
1 tbsp	mixed herbs (parsley, oregano, marjoram)	15 mL
1	pizza dough shell	1
3 oz	cooked ham, cut in julienne	90 g
2 oz	prosciutto, sliced ½ in (1 cm) wide	60 g
3 tbsp	grated Parmesan cheese	45 mL
½ cup	diced mozzarella cheese	125 mL
	juice of ½ lemon	
	salt and pepper	

Preheat oven to 500°F (260°C).

1 Slit leeks from top to bottom twice, leaving 1 in (2.5 cm) intact at base. Wash leeks under cold, running water to remove grit and sand.

2 Place leeks in boiling salted water. Add lemon juice and cook 15 minutes over medium heat.

3 Remove leeks from water and set aside to drain. When cool enough to handle, squeeze out excess liquid, then slice.

4 Heat 2 tbsp (30 mL) oil in frying pan over medium heat. Add leeks and mixed herbs; cook 3 minutes.

5 Spread leeks over pizza dough shell. Add ham and prosciutto; top with cheeses. Season well with pepper and drizzle remaining oil over ingredients.

6 Cook 10 to 12 minutes in oven.

Phyllo Pizza
(6 to 8 servings)

²/₃ cup	melted butter	150 mL
14	sheets phyllo dough, 12 x 16 in (30 x 40 cm)	14
³/₄ cup	grated Parmesan cheese	175 mL
3 tbsp	olive oil	45 mL
2	onions, peeled and thinly sliced	2
2	garlic cloves, peeled, crushed and chopped	2
2 tbsp	chopped fresh basil	30 mL
1 ¼ cups	grated mozzarella cheese	300 mL
4	large tomatoes, cored and sliced ¼ in (5 mm) thick	4
	salt and pepper	

Preheat oven to 375°F (190°C).

1 Brush large baking dish with melted butter. Position first sheet of phyllo dough in bottom and sprinkle with Parmesan cheese. Add next sheet of dough, brush with melted butter and sprinkle with Parmesan. Repeat for remaining sheets of dough.

2 Heat 2 tbsp (30 mL) oil in frying pan over medium heat. Add onions, garlic and basil. Season well and cook 4 minutes. Spoon mixture over top layer of dough.

3 Cover with mozzarella cheese. Top with tomato slices and sprinkle with remaining Parmesan cheese. Drizzle remaining olive oil over tomatoes. Season with pepper.

4 Cook 30 to 40 minutes in oven.

Fresh Mushroom and Bell Pepper Pizza
14-in (36-cm) pizza

1	pizza dough shell	1
²/₃ cup	Fresh Tomato Sauté (see p. 36)	150 mL
1 cup	grated Provolone cheese	250 mL
¼ cup	grated Parmesan cheese	50 mL
16	large fresh mushrooms, cleaned and sliced	16
1	red bell pepper, sliced	1
	extra virgin olive oil	
	salt and pepper	

Preheat oven to 500°F (260°C).

1 Drizzle small amount of olive oil over pizza dough shell. Spread sautéed tomatoes over dough and top with cheeses.

2 Arrange mushrooms and bell pepper over cheese. Season well with salt and pepper.

3 Cook 10 to 12 minutes in oven.

Goat Cheese and Bacon Pizza
14-in (36-cm) pizza

¾ lb	goat cheese	350 g
¼ cup	sour cream	50 mL
¼ cup	chopped pimiento pepper	50 mL
I	pizza dough shell	I
¾ cup	Thick Pizza Sauce (see p. 42)	175 mL
¾ cup	grated Parmesan cheese	175 mL
5	slices crisp cooked bacon, chopped	5
	few drops of Tabasco sauce	
	few drops of Worcestershire sauce	
	salt and pepper	

Preheat oven to 500°F (260°C).

1 Place goat cheese, sour cream, pimiento pepper, and Tabasco and Worcestershire sauces in food processor. Season well and blend to incorporate.

2 Spread cheese mixture over pizza dough shell. Cover with pizza sauce and Parmesan cheese. Season with pepper.

3 Cook 10 to 12 minutes in oven.

4 About 3 minutes before pizza is done, add chopped bacon and complete cooking.

Pizza Romana
14-in (36-cm) pizza

1 cup	Thick Pizza Sauce (see p. 42)	250 mL
1	pizza dough shell	1
1 cup	diced mozzarella cheese	250 mL
¼ tsp	oregano	1 mL
1 tbsp	chopped fresh basil	15 mL
8	anchovy fillets, drained	8
	few drops of olive oil	
	freshly ground pepper	

Preheat oven to 500°F (260°C).

1 Spread pizza sauce over pizza dough shell.

2 Add cheese and seasonings. Arrange anchovy fillets on pizza to resemble spokes of a wheel. Drizzle a few drops of olive oil over pizza and season with pepper.

3 Cook 10 to 12 minutes in oven.

Index